T0146740

EMMAUS ROAD

Stories, Scripture, Hymns, and
Art for the Christian Journey

Rev. Gary M. Schimmer

WESTBOW
PRESS®
A DIVISION OF THOMAS NELSON
& ZONDERVAN

Scripture quotations marked NRSV are taken from the New Revised Standard Version of the Bible, Copyright 1989, by the Division of Christian Education of the National Council of the Churches of Christ in the United States of America. Used by permission. All rights reserved.

WestBow Press books may be ordered through booksellers or by contacting:

WestBow Press
A Division of Thomas Nelson & Zondervan
1663 Liberty Drive
Bloomington, IN 47403
www.westbowpress.com
1 (866) 928-1240

ISBN: 978-1-5127-9382-6 (sc)
ISBN: 978-1-5127-9383-3 (hc)
ISBN: 978-1-5127-9381-9 (e)

Library of Congress Control Number: 2017910927

Print information available on the last page.

WestBow Press rev. date: 7/21/2017

Contents

Introduction

After serving thirty-five years in congregational ministry, I wanted to write about my faith experiences when I prepared for ordained ministry for the Lutheran Church in America (now the Evangelical Lutheran Church in America) at Vanderbilt Divinity School in Nashville, Tennessee, and while I served congregations of that denomination in the Southeast and Midwest areas of the USA.

These moments of faith are offered as a gift for your reflections on the theology and practice of the Christian faith. I hope you will find them helpful for spiritual growth, preaching, and teaching. I hope that they will deepen your faith and draw you closer to God the Father, Son, and Holy Spirit.

Each story has a corresponding Bible verse, an Emmaus Road reflection, a hymn suggestion, and an art suggestion.

Scripture

Each story has a related Bible verse selected from the *New Revised Standard Version of the Bible*.

Stories

Each story is true. I do not betray any confidences when I retell each story. The stories in this book are public information or information known only to me, concerning myself, and I share it freely. No story is taken from any counseling session. The names in each story are changed unless otherwise noted.

An Emmaus Road Reflection

I reflect theologically on each story and Bible verse to deepen the knowledge of the theme for each section and then provide a closing prayer.

Hymns

Unless otherwise noted, hymn suggestions are taken from *Evangelical Lutheran Worship Pew Edition*, © 2006 Evangelical Lutheran Church in America, Augsburg Fortress, Publishers. Each section in this book has only the suggestion for a hymn. I do not copy the music or the text for any hymn.

Art

Each section has an art suggestion corresponding to the theme of the story, Bible verse, or reflection. The master artists were also theologians who conveyed the meaning of the biblical texts. Look at the settings, colors, shading, facial expressions, and other details to understand the theological message of the artist. All suggested works of art are in the public domain and can be found at www.the-athenaeum.org. To make this book affordable, images were published in gray tones. You may look at the color images of these works of art on the Internet at the website mentioned above.

On the cover is Rembrandt's *Supper at Emmaus*, 1648, based on the Gospel of Saint Luke, chapter 24. Notice how Rembrandt painted the risen Christ, with lighter colors surrounding him, to demonstrate his glory. The background is dark, as if Christ is emerging from the tomb. Christ is about to bless and break the bread symbolizing his presence in the sacrament of Holy Communion.

This book is dedicated to my wife, Priscilla. With her love and support, I was able to complete this work and share it with you.

May God the Father, Son, and Holy Spirit bless and keep you.

Rev. Gary M. Schimmer
Lent 2017

SECTION

1

Humor

Again I tell you, it is easier for a camel to go through the eye of a needle than for someone who is rich to enter the kingdom of God.

—Matthew 19:24

A Hymn Forgotten

Sing to him a new song; play skillfully on the strings, with loud shouts.

—Psalm 33:3

While attending divinity school, I was asked to lead the women's Pentecost service at the congregation where I worshipped, taught catechism class, and helped to lead the youth group. With some apprehension, I agreed, knowing that this would be my first time to preach.

In preparation for this service, I worked with a retired pastor who would play the organ for this service. In our phone conversation, we selected several hymns for all to sing.

When I mentioned one of those hymns, the pastor said, "Sing it for me, Gary."

I was shocked and immediately said to him, "On the phone? Sing on the phone?"

Since this pastor had served for many years in a chaplain's position in the mental health field, his reply was probing and challenging. He said, "Gary, people who don't sing are in mental health institutions."

So I sang the hymn on the phone to him, meanwhile thinking that I wasn't a young man needing psychiatric care. I was just a little shy.

The day for the women's Pentecost service arrived. The service was carefully planned, and the chapel was filled with worshippers. The retired pastor who helped me sing and plan the service was at the pipe organ keyboard in the loft at the back of the chapel.

I preached my first sermon, and I was glad when it was over. So I hurriedly walked to the altar to lead in prayer. As I began to pray, I heard a booming voice from the organ loft. The pastor, who was also the organist, shouted, "Gary, you forgot the hymn."

I sheepishly turned around with my face as red as a fire truck. No real harm done. Just a rookie mistake. Calmly I said to all, "We'll sing the next hymn."

Emmaus Road

Even when we're embarrassed and feel silly, God is still with us. He gives us a second chance to try again and chart another course. The Christ who was mocked, derided, and made a fool of on the cross will give us the confidence to move forward again with a renewed faith. Even when we feel we've made fools of ourselves, we can sing again with new and joyful voices to the Lord.

O Lord, when we're foolish, give us a confident faith to live again, serving you.

Hymn: "Thine the Amen," *Evangelical Lutheran Worship* (ELW) #826. Who gets the credit for the blessings of life? Who deserves the praise? Singing "Thine the Amen," we rightly focus our hearts on the God who creates, saves, and sustains us.

Art: *Musical Allegory*, Rembrandt, 1626. What are the instruments being played in this painting? Which person is conducting the musicians? What mood do the facial expressions convey about the music being played? Which musical instruments enrich our singing of praises to the Lord?

Hey, Jesus!

They came to Philip, who was from Bethsaida in Galilee, and said to him, "Sir, we wish to see Jesus."

—John 12:21

The congregation's membership grew rapidly because it was located in a thriving community with many new businesses and housing subdivisions. Young families climbing the corporate ladders were mortgaged to the hilt, enrolled their children in good schools, and looked to worship in welcoming congregations.

It wasn't unusual each Sunday for several new families to show up in the congregation I served. One Sunday a new family, with two little red-haired boys, sat in the pews. As was my practice, I visited new families in their homes to welcome them to the life of my congregation.

When I arrived at this family's house, I rang the doorbell. One of the boys opened the door. Since I was dressed in a clerical collar, he knew that I was somehow connected to the church he and his family had just attended.

With surprise, he shouted out to his mom, "Jesus is here!" I laughed, as did his mom as she greeted me at the door.

The following Sunday, this family came again to Sunday school and worship at my church. Just before Sunday school concluded, I had to use the restroom. I sat in one of the stalls in the men's room.

As if someone wanted to sneak in without being noticed, the door of the men's room opened slowly. But the real story was that the door was heavy and difficult to open, especially for those small boys, who used all their might to gain entry.

They were curious. They looked around the men's room until they saw the feet of someone in the stalls. They peered through the space of my stall to see who might be there, like the knothole children's gangs of old trying to catch a glimpse of a major-league baseball game as they peered through cracks of wood. When they saw me sitting there, they shouted, "Hey, Jesus, are you in there?"

Emmaus Road

Long ago, Jesus was found at a well where a woman came to draw water. He was also found at the seashore with successful fishermen, at a gate where a blind man begged, and at the cross on a hill called Calvary. Teaching, healing, and forgiving, Jesus was found in many places.

As we walk by faith, we believe that Christ's real presence is in, with, and under the bread and wine in Holy Communion. He's present in the hearing of the gospel and in the least of our brothers and sisters who struggle to survive on this earth. We see Jesus in the people of poverty in blighted neighborhoods, in refugee camps where millions have fled to escape war and oppression, and in the homeless who take shelter in stairwells of churches. With eyes of faith, we believe that Christ is present in word and sacrament and in those who are hungry, thirsty, in prison, and all alone.

Loving Savior, grant us faith to see your presence in our lives, and may we be thankful for your surprises of love.

Hymn: "Jesus, Come! For We Invite You," ELW #312. Sung during the season of Epiphany, this hymn implores Jesus to enter our lives as he entered the lives of many people while he walked on this earth. When invited, Jesus comes in unexpected ways to give us the joy of his grace and to awaken our sleepy souls.

Art: *Christ and the Woman of Samaria*, Rembrandt, 1655. Does the way Rembrandt painted Jesus depict him as a teacher? What's the facial expression of the Samaritan woman at the well? Who are the people in the background, and do you think they're astonished at what Jesus is doing?

No Monkey Business

Then God spoke all these words: "I am the Lord your God, who brought you out of the land of Egypt, out of the house of slavery; you shall have no other gods before me."
—Exodus 20:1–3

What can we do to keep the attention of children in Sunday school? A new Bible curriculum may include the latest technology with fast-paced songs and flashy lessons to nurture faith.

But before the latest technology hit the classroom, we used flannel boards, brightly colored Bible story leaflets, and songs with hand motions. (Remember the old Sunday school song "The Wise Man Built His House upon the Rock?") And some Sunday school teachers even tried show-and-tell in class to capture the attention of restless children.

Danny was an energetic five-year-old in his Sunday school class. He watched and listened carefully to the students who brought a toy or two to show in class. A little girl told everyone about her stuffed monkey. It was cute and cuddly.

As she returned to her seat, Danny asked if he could see her stuffed animal. He took that stuffed monkey and didn't hug it and treat it gently. Instead, Danny threw it across the room as if he were throwing a ball across the playground. Fellow students and the teacher were surprised as he hurled that cute stuffed monkey that day in class. They couldn't believe what Danny had done.

After the class settled down, another student, Mikey, took his turn at show-and-tell. He brought a comb and a watch. When he completed his presentation, Danny piped up again and asked Mikey if he could see his watch. Mikey had a quick response: "No way, José! I saw what you did to that monkey."

Emmaus Road

There are moments in life to say *no* clearly. Children are taught to say *no* when strangers offer them rides home. On one hand, God shouted a divine *no* in the Ten Commandments. To keep life in order, to love and care for our neighbors, and to keep the Almighty as the most important presence in our lives, God set boundaries for us. Within these boundaries are blessings, while moving beyond them brings despair, pain, and hopelessness. So we say *no* to those acts that tempt us to place God second in our lives. And we say *no* to murder, adultery, theft, bearing false witness, and coveting.

Martin Luther believed that if we would obey the first commandment to place God above everything else, we would also obey the remaining commandments. Now that's a tall order, considering our sinful human condition. But the God who first promised to be our God and to be on our side is the same God who forgives us and gives us the Holy Spirit so our light of faith shines in this world. With divine help, we can say *no* to monkey business.

Eternal God, we thank you for the Ten Commandments, which guide our lives in this world and provide knowledge of your good and gracious will.

Hymn: "Let Us Ever Walk with Jesus," ELW #802. Which path will guide us to truth? Walking with Jesus, we have a faithful companion as we face daily struggles. Jesus will finally lead us to joy and raise us up to daily renewal in his name.

Art: *Moses Destroying the Tablets*, Rembrandt, 1659. What is the expression on the face of Moses? What do you think was on his mind and heart as he received these commandments from God? What was his mood as he raised them and began to throw them down to destroy them?

Pizza and a Movie

Then he poured water into a basin and began to wash the disciples' feet.

—John 13:5a

They said they came from Hollywood, where they worked to film the 1960s sitcom *Petticoat Junction*. They landed in the small Georgia town where I was the pastor of the Lutheran congregation. It always puzzled me how these two filmmakers left the glamour of Hollywood to live and work in a town and country setting in the foothills of the north Georgia mountains. I met them as they worked for a major pizza chain. They were filming community events and then inviting the community to the local pizza restaurant for dinner and a movie.

Somehow I got the idea of filming *A Day in the Life of a Pastor,* starring yours truly. I approached these two men and shared the idea, and they agreed. I thought this would be a fun way to involve not only myself but the congregation too, and perhaps it would be a new way to share the gospel ministry. Who could turn down a pizza and a movie, especially when you and your friends are featured in the film?

So *A Day in the Life of a Pastor* began filming at the parsonage early one morning. I was shown dressing with my clerical collar while a Willie Nelson song played in the background. I then sat down at the desk in my home office and pretended to work on a sermon. We were off to a good start.

Next we staged a counseling session in the church office, and then I was filmed driving onto the parking lot of the local hospital to make a pastoral call.

That afternoon, as I picked up my daughter from middle school, I said how pleasant it was to see her and how orderly the students were as they left the classrooms for the day. However, I spoke too soon. As my daughter was filmed getting into my car, two boys fought in the background. So much for a peaceful afternoon.

Then it was back to the parsonage. My wife, daughter, and I sat in the den. I pulled out my guitar and began to play. But it was not my fingers playing the music. Sorry, we dubbed in Segovia. What was I thinking? I faked it. It was reality TV at its worst.

The final scene filmed was on Sunday morning. The worship service was over. As members walked out of the red doors of the stately, gray stone church building, they were filmed. When they realized they were on camera, some members waved *hello*, and some made weird faces. It was all in good fun.

I had no idea that I would be a forerunner of reality TV. (Just kidding.) Nonetheless, as this feature film played one evening at the local pizza restaurant, we ate, drank, and watched *A Day in the Life of a Pastor*. It was pastoral ministry in action. It was "Pizza Vision." ("Pizza Vision" was a publicity plan of Domino's in the 1970s.)

Emmaus Road

Jesus's disciples continued his ministry as they healed and preached in his name. They served those in need. They traveled to spread the good news of a loving Savior. Some even faced gruesome deaths for their witness to Christ.

On Maundy Thursday, the Christian church traditionally keeps its ancient practice of washing feet. It is a reenactment of what Jesus did to teach humility and service. As we participate in this rite, we feel strengthened to follow in Christ's way to serve a hurting and broken world. We surprise the world with Christ's love as we comfort the afflicted, feed the hungry, and provide shelter to the homeless. We become advocates for the poor and those who have no voice in the political arena.

The ordained clergy and lay people are all baptized in Christ. We are all priests and fellow believers. We share a common ministry to wash the feet of others as Christ did long ago.

Gracious God, raise up leaders for your holy church and strengthen the faith of all who follow you.

Hymn: "Christ Be Our Light," ELW #715. With this hymn, we sing of our deep desire to follow in Christ's way as true and loving servants in this world.

Art: *Christ Washing the Disciples' Feet*, Jacopo Tintoretto, 1548–1549. Notice the halos surrounding the heads of Christ and his disciples. In this painting, can you identify which disciple is having his feet washed? What are the other disciples doing as Jesus is washing the feet of one of his disciples? Does this painting help you reflect upon the meaning of Christian discipleship?

Lights Out

Live as children of light.

—Ephesians 5:8b

I have enjoyed doing children's sermons since I began my ordained ministry decades ago. Each Sunday I talked to children about the meaning of one of the Bible verses from the lectionary. I always tried to make one point in my talks. I used signs, toys, pictures, and movements to illustrate my message.

One Sunday I talked about Jesus's message for people to be the light of the world. Now that concept was not easy to communicate to children because it was a metaphor. Nonetheless, I gave it a try. I gave each child a little flashlight. They aimed their lights at each other and on the walls of the church building. I emphasized that Jesus wants us to be the light of the world. That meant that we are to love him and others. So we are to let that love of Christ shine in our lives.

On Monday I received an email from a father whose child had listened to my sermon. It seems that the parents of this child had asked him what he learned from the children's sermon. The parents hoped that their child would talk about loving Jesus and others. But instead the little one said to his parents, "Pastor Schimmer wants us to keep all the lights on in the house."

Poking a little fun at me, the father wrote, "Pastor Schimmer, I will now be sending you my electric bills." So much for trying to explain to a biblical metaphor to three- and four-year-old children.

Emmaus Road

The red, green, and yellow lights of a traffic signal make for safe travel. The flashing blue lights of a police car caution us to slow down and finally stop our vehicles. The white, streaming light from a lighthouse provides safe harbor for a vessel at sea. So when Jesus used the metaphor *the light of the world*, what does that mean for us? He called us to bear good fruit for him in this world. Our faith in this world is not to remain hidden. It is for all to see. We are to bear witness to Christ's love, and that means service and even sacrifice.

A flash of light provides guidance. A flash of light illumines pathways. A flash of light reveals what was once hidden. Likewise, as we let our light of faith shine in this world, we guide those sitting in spiritual darkness. We illuminate pathways so others see what is true and just. We uncover the deep and deceptive evil in this world so that it can be defeated, and peace will once again flourish.

Holy Spirit, may we be lights of faith to shine in this world and reflect the love of Christ.

Hymn: "I Want to Walk as a Child of the Light," ELW #815. Children love to sing this hymn about their divine calling to live by following Jesus and to let his love shine in all that they do, think, and say.

Art: *Creation of Light*, John Richmond, 1826. Describe the anthropomorphic image of God in this painting. Does God appear to be an elderly, feeble man, or is God depicted as a strong and powerful person? Does God appear to make room for light with the sweeping motion of his hand? Describe the image of light in this painting. Is light streaming through the darkness like rays of sun breaking through dark clouds? Does the creation of light by God provide hope in the midst of darkness and chaos?

Hand Signals

Jesus said, "Let the little children come to me, and do not stop them; for it is to such as these that the kingdom of heaven belongs."

—Matthew 19:14b

Receiving Holy Communion is one of the spiritual stepping stones in the Christian faith. In the early Christian Church, even infants communed by tasting drops of wine that the priest placed on their tongues. Centuries later, that early Christian practice changed, and now children in the first grade or in upper grades commune for the first time.

It was the practice of my congregation to offer children their first Holy Communion in the third grade, as I recall. They received instruction before they received this sacrament. On the other hand, younger children still came forward at the moment of Holy Communion in worship for a blessing. I would place my hand on their heads and say the appropriate words for a blessing.

But children like to grow up fast. They like to do what their older brothers and sisters do. Such was the case with one little child in my congregation. His older brother had already received his first Communion, and that younger brother wanted to have what his older brother received at the altar rail—the bread and the wine.

So one Sunday, as this little child knelt at the altar rail with his older brother and parents, he did something peculiar. As I got ready to lay my hand on his head and say the blessing, he put one hand on his head and reached out his other hand to receive the communion wafer.

I was shocked and yet pleasantly amused at the same time. His mother saw what was happening and gently took her son's hand from his head so I could give him the blessing. And even though this little child did not receive the bread and wine that Sunday, he still received a welcome from Christ as I laid my hand on his head and reminded him that the Lord will bless and keep him.

Emmaus Road

We eat the bread and drink the wine in Holy Communion, believing that Christ is truly present with his promise for forgiveness, life, and salvation. I have often thought that children should receive the sacrament of Holy Communion as they did centuries ago. After all, it is in faith that we joyfully receive this sacrament. Our reception of Christ's own body and blood is really not dependent on our knowledge of this mystery. Certainly, as a child grows, there needs to be catechesis to mature in the knowledge of the Christian faith and its practices.

Eternal God, fill us with grace as we feast at your table and help us to hold onto your promise for faith and life in this holy meal.

Hymn: "Draw Us in the Spirit's Tether," ELW #470. It is Christ who invites us to Holy Communion. Communing, we experience his presence in faith. As we eat and drink at the Lord's table, we are united in faith to him and to others in the body of Christ.

Art: *Christ Blessing the Children*, Lucas Cranach the Younger, date unknown. In this painting, what is Jesus doing to bless the children? What is the reaction of the children to Jesus? Describe the facial expressions of the mothers.

SECTION

2

Surprise

Then their eyes were opened, and they recognized him.
—Luke 24:31a

Preach On, Brother!

If I proclaim the gospel, this gives me no ground for boasting, for an obligation is laid on me, and woe to me if I do not proclaim the gospel.

—1 Corinthians 9:16

As I began my ordained ministry, I wanted to do my best with preaching. To build my confidence and skill, I went to church late one Saturday evening to practice my sermon for Sunday morning. I did not lock the front doors of the church; it was the custom of this congregation to leave the church doors unlocked day and night.

I stood in the pulpit, preaching if it were a real Sunday morning service. Halfway through my sermon, I was startled as the doors to the nave were flung open, and a stranger walked down the center aisle and sat in the front pew right in front of me. I stopped for a moment, and then he shouted, "Preach on, brother!"

He was a front-pew cheerleader dressed in a white T-shirt and blue jeans; he had short brown hair and was of average height and weight. His shout encouraged me to keep on preaching as if I were preaching at a revival and wanted to stir the emotions of the crowd.

But I did not heed his encouragement. Instead I asked him, "Where do you live? How can I help you?" In my momentary shock, I forgot to ask him his name first. He said that he needed a place to sleep for the evening and wondered if he could spend the night in the church. But when I suggested that he go to the police department for help, he jumped up from his seat and dashed down that center aisle, never to be seen by me again.

No more front-pew cheers. No more encouragement to preach on and proclaim the word of God. He disappeared as swiftly as he had entered, and I vowed, from that moment forward, never to practice my sermons in the church on late Saturday nights.

Emmaus Road

When Jesus preached in front of his family and friends, the synagogue must have been packed. They saw the child Jesus as he played with friends in the streets. They watched him learn the carpenter's trade from his father. They worshipped and studied the Hebrew scriptures with the son of Mary and Joseph. He was just one of the guys in Nazareth but felt the call to preach and teach the faith they all knew.

As he preached in the synagogue, all were astonished at what he said. His insights were inspiring. He claimed that he fulfilled the words of the prophets. His preaching would never be forgotten.

Saint Paul believed that he was called to preach the good news of Jesus Christ after his Damascus road experience. He was determined never to preach false myths or the message of mystery religions but to proclaim Christ crucified for the salvation for all.

So preach on, brothers and sisters! Preach the gospel. Stir up the hearts of the faithful with challenges to follow the Lord faithfully and walk along paths of light and life. Tell them to reject sin and the snares of the evil one. Remind them of the grace of the Lord Jesus Christ for forgiveness and to rely on the Holy Spirit to bear good fruit.

Holy Father, you illuminate our pathways in a world of confusion. Keep us spiritually focused on your word to gladden our hearts.

Hymn: "Alleluia! Sing to Jesus," ELW #392. We not only preach the gospel—we sing it too. Singing this hymn is like preaching a sermon with poetry as the Lord is praised.

Art: *Saint Paul Preaching in Athens*, Raffaello Sanzio da Urbino (Raphael), 1515. What is the reaction to Saint Paul's preaching? Where is his location for preaching? Does this painting give you the impression that the gospel is for the world?

Asleep

In that region there were shepherds living in the fields,
keeping watch over their flock by night.

—Luke 2:8

One Christmas Eve, everything was ready for the late night service, which
was to start an hour before midnight. The Christmas tree was lit. So were
the candles on the altar. Each worshipper had a candle to light while singing
"Silent Night, Holy Night." The red poinsettias adorned the chancel, and
the white paraments on the altar and pulpit added to the splendor of the
evening.

All went well with the service. Voices blended together when hymns were
sung. The reading of Christ's birth from Saint Luke's Gospel joyfully
touched our hearts. The choir, which had practiced many hours for this
service, sang beautifully. I thought nothing could disrupt the peaceful mood
of this service.

But I was wrong. When it came time to gather the offering, I assumed
the ushers would dutifully collect the gifts from God's people. I paid no
attention to them since I was busily preparing the wine and bread for
distribution during the Holy Communion part of the service.

Just as the organist began playing the offertory hymn, however, I looked up
and expected to see the ushers walking down the center aisle toward the
altar with offering plates in hand to present to God. But they were not in
their usual place. I looked a bit further, and much to my surprise, I saw the

ushers all sleeping on the back row of the church. They missed the moment for the offering—on Christmas Eve, no less.

When the organist completed the offertory hymn, I smiled and said again, "We will now receive the offering."

By that time the ushers had awakened and began collecting the gifts from the people of God. With a second chance for them to keep watch, the ushers completed their task. And no real harm was done.

I guess the late hour, the peaceful mood of the service, the sweet hymns, and the calm voice of the preacher contributed to the sleepiness of the four men on the back row. I was happy that we even had ushers for a late night Christmas Eve service. It was difficult to get them. The head usher for that service even had to draft a volunteer from the congregation, who wore a black tuxedo with tails and white tennis shoes. Before the service, he had been parking cars at a resort on the Gulf Coast. On his way home, he stopped at the church for the Christmas Eve service. Little did he know that he would be dashing down the center aisle of the church as he had dashed to park cars at that luxurious resort.

Keep awake! Keep watch! The Lord is coming, and so is the time for the offering.

Emmaus Road

Jacob slept on a rock, and God gave him a vision of angels descending to earth and then ascending to heaven. While he slept, God told Joseph to take Mary as his wife. As Saint Peter slumbered, God set a vision in his mind about what food was clean and unclean. Sleep is good. Our bodies need rest. And God can communicate messages to us even when we are fast asleep. Sweet dreams.

Gracious Lord, grant us peace when our hearts are troubled and gentle rest when we slumber.

Hymn: "Where Shepherds Lately Knelt," Concordia Publishing House, 1986. What was the mood of the shepherds when the angel announced to them the birth of the Messiah? As Rev. Jaroslav Vajda wrote the lyrics of this hymn, he reflected upon the mood of the shepherds when they knelt before the divine infant in the arms of Mary. Were their hearts filled with joy at this sight? As we sing this hymn, we reflect upon the wonder and mystery of the Word made flesh.

Art: *The Adoration of the Shepherds,* El Greco, 1610. Are the angels above celebrating the birth of the Messiah while the angel at the manger is in humble adoration of God's Son? What is the mood of the shepherds? Notice the brilliance of color surrounding the infant Jesus and Mary, his mother. What does this brilliance indicate?

Ambush

> So out of the ground the Lord God formed every animal
> of the field and every bird of the air, and brought them to
> the man to see what he could call them.
>
> —Genesis 2:19a

Visiting congregational members in their homes was one of my priorities in my first call for ministry. So I called on one member to visit him on his farm just outside a small town. He raised chickens, rabbits, pigs, and cows. He also had a big black-and-brown dog. This dog was a mutt, could outrun a rabbit, and liked to ambush his prey.

I drove to this man's farm one sunny afternoon. As I got out of my car and walked to the front porch of the house, it happened. That farm dog darted out from the bushes and ran straight toward my legs. That big mutt, about the size of a German shepherd, clamped his jaws on my left foot and held on until his owner came to the front door and called him off. The dog's teeth left an impression on my shoe but did not get to flesh and blood. Thank goodness that this ambush was not as shocking as one might think.

A bit shaken, I walked into the farmhouse and sat down for a moment of conversation with my congregational member. We then walked outside to his backyard. Sure enough, there were chickens roaming, pigs in a pen, rabbits in a cage, and cows grazing in the field. It was a backyard farm.

A few months later, I called this member again to make another visit. But this time I was prepared. As I walked up to his white frame farmhouse, I looked at the bushes to see if the dog was there. In a flash, he dashed at me again and tried to bite me on the same foot, but it was to no avail. I wore my thick-soled, heavy-duty leather work boots from summers spent working at a manufacturing plant. This time the dog got a different taste in his mouth—no, not the taste of some soft leather shoe but the taste of worn, rugged, dirty leather. I had my revenge. Unscathed, unshaken, and ready for another lesson about the farm animals God created, I made my way once again into my member's house.

Emmaus Road

In the creation story in Genesis, God fashioned all the creatures of the earth and brought them to Adam to name. We can just imagine the surprised look on Adam's face as God showed him giraffes with long necks, or short and stocky pigs, or brightly colored birds. It was God's parade of animals, with sights and sounds delightful to this first man, whom God had created out of the dust of the ground. God created the animal kingdom, and Adam named all the animals God set before him. Like Adam, we behold the wonder of God's creation and are called to care for all creatures that God has made, even farm dogs who ambush strangers with sharp teeth and frightening growls.

God of creation, help us to care for this good earth and all its creatures to honor your glorious name.

Hymn: "God of the Sparrow," ELW #740. This hymn calls all of creation—the animals on earth, the celestial bodies, and people of every time and place—to stand in awe of what God has done and give thanks and praise.

Art: *Paradise*, Jan Brueghel the Younger, circa 1620. What animals in this painting can you identify? Do they all seem to be at peace in paradise? How well do we care for God's good creation?

Snake Handler

See, I have given you authority to tread on snakes and
scorpions, and over all the power of the enemy; and nothing
will hurt you.

—Luke 10:19

I arrived at church early Sunday morning to unlock the doors, turn on the
lights, make sure the worship folders were on the usher's table, and check
the altar to see that everything was in order for Holy Communion.

But as I began to unlock the church door and pull it open, two yellow-
ringed, black snakes fell from on top of the door to the ground just below
my feet. These startled snakes moved like flashes of lightning and scurried
into the church narthex.

What was I to do? Church members would be showing up shortly for the
early morning service. Would I have to advise them to watch their feet
because these uninvited creatures might slither under the pews? Should I
ask if there was a herpetologist in the house?

Snake handling was not one my gifts or skills. So I thought of the next
best thing—the broom in the hall closet. I would simply take that broom
and whisk those uninvited guests away. So I ran to the closet, gripped that
broom like a knight taking up his sword for battle, and ran back to the
narthex for a showdown with the snakes.

Whisk. Whisk. Whisk. A few quick swipes with the broom, and those
snakes swiftly headed out the narthex doors and across the concrete walk

and disappeared into the brown bark packed around the bushes on the front lawn of the church.

Those two snakes were handled with ease. They returned to their natural, cozy habitats. All was well once again. And no attendees had to prove their faith that day in church by treading on those two uninvited creatures, who had slithered away to safety.

Emmaus Road

The serpent in the garden of Eden enticed Eve to doubt God's word and eat of the tree of knowledge of good and evil. Eve ate, and so did Adam. Paradise was lost. Divine boundaries were broken. Disobedience entered into perfection, and humanity was lost in sin and corruption.

I first heard of snake handlers in a class taught by one of my professors at divinity school. He said that he attended a worship service in eastern Tennessee, where Christians gathered, and one of the guitar players for the service had a snake slithering on his guitar.

When Jesus spoke of treading on snakes and scorpions as a display of faith, he was speaking metaphorically. Faithful Christians live with confidence in God to protect them in the midst of danger. Jesus's words do not literally command us to place ourselves in danger by handling snakes to test God and to prove our worthiness to him.

While in the wilderness, the Israelites were bitten by poisonous snakes. God told Moses to lift high a serpent on a pole, and all who looked upon it would be saved. Jesus, too, was lifted high on a cross, and all who look to him in faith are saved from the threatening dangers of their sins.

O God, you heal our diseases by your gracious power. Bring healing and wholeness to all who suffer.

Hymn: "Healer of Our Every Ill," ELW #612. We sing of the healing that God provides in the midst of danger and fears. It is God who gives us peace beyond what the world can give.

Art: *Moses and the Brazen Serpent*, Peter Paul Rubens, 1609–1610. Why is Moses pointing to the serpent on the pole? What is the reaction of those who look at the serpent? Do we look to the Lord for healing in time of need?

No-frills Stewardship

> Each of you must give as you have made up your mind, not
> reluctantly or under compulsion, for God loves a cheerful
> giver.
>
> —2 Corinthians 9:7

I learned something about stewardship that day when one of my faithful
church members, Bobby, took me to visit another member of the
congregation who lived in an assisted living facility.

As we walked into this senior member's room, he was lying in bed. He had
white, neatly cut hair. He looked frail and appeared a little over five feet tall.

His room had the bare essentials: a hospital bed, a chest of drawers, and a
night table with a lamp. I do not recall any pictures hanging on the wall or
a window for sunshine to brighten up his room.

Bobby introduced me to him, and we had cordial conversation. I learned that he
once lived in South America and in a couple of southern states. He spent many
years working in the cotton industry and apparently accumulated some wealth.

Following our conversation, I gave him Holy Communion, which he
appreciated. Then Bobby opened the door to this senior's closet, gathered up his
dirty clothes, and put them in a bag so that he could launder them at his home.

But before we left that day, Bobby had one more matter in mind. Without any
hesitation, Bobby asked this senior for a check for the church. Bobby wrote
it, and this senior signed it without reluctance. He seemed rather pleased
that he had someone to help him make this gift for congregational ministry.

When this moment of giving took place, I was pleasantly surprised. I never thought this visit would end with check writing. It never came to my mind that asking for gifts to support the church's ministry could be so straightforward. It did not take a six-week stewardship campaign with letters, talks, preaching, and Bible study to work up to asking, in this case, for this senior's treasure. It only took Bobby, with his faith and a good relationship with this senior, to encourage a gift for ministry.

Emmaus Road

Christian stewardship is not a one-shot deal. It is a lifestyle in which every moment is lived with a generous and grateful heart, thanking God, who gives us all that we need to live. We believe that God is the owner of all creation and that we are the caretakers of all his abundant gifts.

Saint Paul provided guidelines for Christian giving. We are to give cheerfully, not begrudgingly. God frees us to give of our time, talent, and treasure. God strengthens us to care for creation. Created in God's image, we reflect his lavish giving in a world that desperately needs grace and mercy.

Lord of the harvest, we give you boundless praise and thanksgiving for providing our daily bread. Help us to share with those who cry out from hunger and thirst.

Hymn: "God, Whose Giving Knows No Ending," ELW #678. The poetry of this hymn beautifully speaks of God's endless blessings and our call to be his servants, who share what was first given to us.

Art: *The Widow's Mite*, Gabriel Metzu, 1650–1652. Does Jesus seem to be teaching a lesson in this painting? What gives us this indication? What is the facial expression on the widow? Does she seem humble? Does this painting call us to reflect upon the nature of our giving in response to God's grace?

Generous Practice

Let the elders who rule well be considered worthy of double honor.

—1 Timothy 5:17

I advertised in the local newspaper that I had a piano for sale. My wife and I bought it when we were first married. One man responded to this notice and made an appointment to come to our home to check it out.

He rang the doorbell. We greeted him. He took off his shoes before he entered. He introduced himself and said that he was looking to purchase a piano for his daughter's birthday present.

He sat at our piano and played beautifully. He was impressed with the instrument. We agreed on a price for the transaction, and then he said he would return in a few days with a truck to load his daughter's birthday present.

Before he left that day, we learned that he was a member of the Seventh-day Adventist Church. I shared that I had been ordained as a minister in the Lutheran Church some thirty years ago.

When he returned to pick up the piano, he wrote a check. But when I read the amount on the check, I was surprised.

I said, "Hey, you gave me ten percent more than what I asked."

He replied, "It says in the Bible that we should honor our elders."

I smiled. I had not known anyone who would be so generous about a small business deal. He took that Bible verse in 1 Timothy seriously and believed that elders were worthy of honor or compensation; he honored me with a very generous check for his daughter's new piano.

Emmaus Road

Order and structure were needed when the Christian church emerged in the first century. Saint Paul instructed his young pastor, Timothy, on many topics, including the qualifications of bishops and deacons and faith practices for the Christian community. One such practice was to honor those in ecclesiastical authority. Thus elders who ruled well were to be doubly honored or compensated for this church ministry.

The man who bought my piano had a heart for church leaders. He took off his shoes when he entered my house. He knew scripture. He was kind and respectful. He paid me well above the asking price. He gave from the abundance God had first given to him.

O God of love, you give us an abundance of gifts. May we use them in your service so others may know of your generous goodness.

Hymn: "We Give Thee but Thine Own," ELW #686. God is the giver. We are the recipients of his bounties. In all matters, we dedicate our lives to him who first gives to us.

Art: *The Tribute Money*, Rembrandt, 1635. Who are the people gathered around Jesus? Notice how Rembrandt used light and darkness to emphasize Jesus's holiness. Does it appear that this is another teaching moment in Jesus's life? What was Jesus's message about giving to God and to Caesar?

Big Man, Big Trouble

Let every person be subject to the governing authorities; for there is no authority except from God, and those authorities that exist have been instituted by God.

—Romans 13:1

The building of my first church was small and seated only about a hundred worshippers, but the walls were thick, gray granite. My small and cozy church office was next to the chancel. As I sat there one afternoon, colorful rays of light streamed through the stained glass window. I felt at peace as I prepared my sermon. I always left my church office door open so I could hear if anyone entered the church through the doors of the nave.

I was startled when I heard a cracking sound from the doors to the nave. The sound of the door opening was not soft and normal. It was heavy and disturbing with the cracking of wood. Someone walked into the church building and leaned so hard against the wooden nave doors that one of them was damaged.

My heart began to pound as I sensed trouble. I jumped up from my chair, peered into the nave, and saw no one. I hurriedly walked down the center aisle of the nave, carefully took a peak into the small narthex, and again saw no one. I then opened the big, red front door of the church building, and I saw him. Tall and muscular, he staggered down the sidewalk as if overcome with a few too many alcoholic beverages.

I locked the front doors of the church, ran back to my office, and called the police. When the police arrived a few moments later, I stood at the red door of the church to see what would happen. The police officer tried to talk to this big man, but he wanted no part of it. When he pushed the officer away, a wrestling match began. They both fell hard on the concrete sidewalk. The officer finally prevailed and had the big man handcuffed. The big man was apprehended, and all was calm again.

But that frightening incident unfortunately changed church policy. Since the congregation's beginnings in the 1930s, the front doors of the church were always unlocked. But with the rise of crime and the potential harm to anyone alone in that stately granite building, church leaders decided to keep the doors locked. No more people entering the church during the week on their lunch hours for prayer and meditation. No more moments of silence for visitors during the week, sitting in the nave while enjoying the stained glass artwork of Jesus praying in the garden of Gethsemane displayed above the altar. How sad but true, and it all happened because of a big man who caused some big trouble.

Emmaus Road

Laws are intended for the good order of society. Break them, and there are consequences. Obey them, and there is peace. God gave his chosen people the Ten Commandments to direct them to love him and their neighbors. Saint Paul wrote about obeying the governing authorities who are called to keep order and enforce the laws of the land.

Throughout history, as we know, some governments have been oppressive. But governments can also seek justice, administer punishment, and grant pardons and mercy. God not only rules in the sacred realm but also in the secular realm, with good government protecting the rights and freedom of its citizens.

God of mercy, bless all who are in prison. Grant them repentant hearts and peace for new life in your Son, Jesus Christ, our Lord.

Hymn: "This Is My Song," ELW #887. We implore the God of the nations to bless our land with peace and to have his will done among us.

Art: *Saint Paul in Prison*, Rembrandt, 1627. What is Saint Paul's mood? Why does he have a sword if he is in prison? What do you think he is writing? Could he be pondering the purpose of governing authorities? Does this painting encourage us to think about justice in our land?

Bus Ticket

And God is able to provide you with every blessing in abundance, so that by always having enough of everything, you may share abundantly in every good work.

—2 Corinthians 9:8

It was Saturday night. I did not have a date. I had eaten supper and did not want to hit the books to prepare for divinity school classes on Monday. I guess there was nothing better to do than to load my dirty clothes into my 1964 aqua Fire Chief and head to the nearest coin-operated Laundromat. I even took a book along to read and pass the time.

I sat by myself in that Laundromat on Saturday night until a young man walked in. He had no laundry basket with dirty clothes. He was short, slim, had greased-backed hair, and seemed to be no threat to me. He shared with me his hard-luck story. He said his mother was ill in Mississippi, and he did not have enough money to buy a bus ticket to visit her.

I was naïvely quick to react. I told him that once my clothes were dry, I would drive him to the downtown bus station and buy him a ticket. I thought I was doing the right thing. I was doing my Christian duty. I thought, "I won't let him pull the wool over my eyes by just giving him some cash and telling him to hit the road." After all, wasn't helping my neighbor in need the Christlike action?

So after my clothes were dry, folded, and put in my laundry basket, off we went to the bus station. I did as I promised. I bought him the bus ticket. Feeling good about myself, I drove back to my apartment with a clean conscience and clean clothes. I felt proud that I could help this man who was down on his luck. I felt he was legitimately in need and not someone who had tried to bilk me out of cash so he could have a good time.

The next morning I rose early, got dressed, and went to the downtown Lutheran church where I worshipped, taught confirmation class, and assisted with the liturgy. But as I drove past that Laundromat, I was surprised. There he was. The man for whom I had bought that bus ticket was walking down the street. He never boarded that bus to Mississippi to visit his sick mother. He most likely turned in that ticket, got the cash, and had his Saturday night fling. I was hoodwinked, cheated, and deceived. He was street-smart, and I was not wise to his ways. He was one of the least of my brothers, but he was also a con artist who fooled anyone who bought his story about his sick mother.

Emmaus Road

Jesus, help me, for I have been tricked! I trusted a man I had never met before. I thought I was serving my neighbor in need, but I was just feeding his bad habit. But do I keep trusting the homeless, the down-and-out, the alcoholics, and the street people? How do I know that my sacrifices for them are appreciated? Do I ever say *no* to the least of the people who come my way?

All I can do is to trust Jesus and discern his will when I meet the poor, the homeless, and those seeking help. When I sense those who are in real need, may I be generous and compassionate. When I decide that I am being cheated, may I be forgiving and guide those people along right pathways.

Compassionate God, as you reached out to the poor and marginalized, so help me to follow in your way and offer Christian charity.

Hymn: "Praise and Thanksgiving," ELW #689. We give God praise and glory for the harvests of the field and pray for him to give us wisdom to share so that everyone, everywhere, may share in his bounty.

Art: *The Feeding of the Five Thousand*, Carl Van Loo, 1733. Who are the men standing nearest to Jesus? Do they appear to be careful listeners? What kinds of food are being distributed? Does Jesus appear to be teaching in this painting? Does this painting lead us to ponder how well we share with the hungry, including those we suspect might be trying to deceive us?

Gentle Touch

She came up behind him and touched the fringe of his clothes, and immediately her hemorrhage stopped.

—Luke 8:44

On occasion I was a substitute chaplain at a physical rehabilitation hospital where visits took place on Sunday afternoons. On one of those occasions, I walked into the hospital's lobby as I normally did and went to the security desk. Behind that desk stood the security guard. She was fairly tall, slender, and had dark, wavy hair. She looked official in her uniform with a long-sleeved, light blue shirt, dark blue pants, silver badge, and a handgun in her holster. She was ready to do her job and offer protection in time of danger.

We had a brief and pleasant conversation. She told me that she was experiencing some emotional distress and said that I should keep her in prayer. Since I was also dressed in my uniform, black suit with a clerical collar, she expected more from me than prayer. I mean she must have thought that I could somehow give her some immediate relief from her turmoil.

Here is the reason. As I began to sign in at the security desk, I felt a tug at the bottom of one of my pants legs. I looked, and there was that security guard tugging at the hem of my pants.

Startled, I asked, "What are you doing?"

Humbly she replied, "You know, it says in the Bible if you just touch the hem of his garment."

I quickly said, "But I am not Jesus." Nonetheless, her gentle touch gave her hope of healing from her despair.

As I reflected on that incident, I should have been more sensitive to her needs. I should have taken another moment to talk with her, listen to her, and offer prayer and consolation. Her faith was strong. But her touch shocked me. It surprised me, and I was quick to avoid a potentially embarrassing moment. I needed to remain calm and open to the opportunity to share the love of Christ.

Emmaus Road

Touch is important for healing. When we pray for someone who is gravely ill, we touch that person's forehead, make the sign of the cross with oil, and pray for healing. When we install or ordain someone to ministry or confirm a youth, we lay hands on that person and pray for the power of the Holy Spirit to stir up their lives of faith. In baptism, we gently hold the baby and touch the forehead with the water of life as that child is welcomed into the body of Christ.

That security guard who gently touched the hem of my pants wanted healing. She yearned for that healing touch from the Holy Spirit to make her life whole again. A gentle and appropriate touch conveys a spirit of peace and a moment of love.

O Lord, let your wings of love embrace all who struggle with the illnesses of life and restore them to health.

Hymn: "Thy Holy Wings," ELW #613. Using the metaphor of a protective mother hen, we sing to God for safety and care.

Art: *Healing of the Lame Man*, Raphael, 1515. Who are the two disciples in the middle of this painting? (See Acts 3.) Is touch important for healing? Are words also important? What is the mood of the crowd as this miracle is taking place? Have you experienced moments of healing touch?

SECTION

3

Justice

Wash yourselves; make yourselves clean; remove the evil
of your doings from before my eyes; cease to do evil, learn
to do good; seek justice, rescue the oppressed, defend the
orphan, plead for the widow.

—Isaiah 1:16–17

Time to March

> But as for you, return to your God, hold fast to love and justice, and wait continually for your God.
>
> —Hosea 12:6

I was a teenager in 1965, when Martin Luther King, Jr. led the civil rights protest march from Selma to Montgomery, Alabama. I knew it had something to do with equality, but I never fully understood its meaning and the great impact it had on our country back then.

After the election of Donald Trump as president of the United States, there have been protests. Some have been as peaceful as the protests of Mohandas Gandhi or King himself. Unfortunately some have been vulgar and violent and involved destruction of property. How I yearn for protesters to protest in a nonviolent way!

While in divinity school at Vanderbilt University in 1978, the Davis Cup was scheduled to be played on campus with a team from South Africa. That country was in the midst of racial tension over the policy of apartheid. Vanderbilt faculty and students marched in front of Kirkland Hall in protest of this tennis match on campus. I took part. At the divinity school, there was much discussion about the effectiveness of a protest march. Students' opinions were divided on this topic. My participation in this march was my first public display of protest against an unjust political policy.

A few years later, I was the chairman of my synod's Social (Justice) Ministry Committee. I recall that the Lutheran Church in America released a social statement on capital punishment. This statement was a guideline to help Christians reflect ethically and theologically upon this social issue. As chairman, I took the opportunity to march in protest against capital punishment from the state capitol to the Martin Luther King, Jr. Center in Atlanta. As I recall, there were many groups participating in the march. I can't remember them all. But I do remember that all marchers seemed passionate about ridding our country of what they believed was cruel and unusual punishment.

Emmaus Road

While in the wilderness, the Israelites protested against Moses. God's chosen people were tired. They felt that they would not reach the promised land, flowing with milk and honey. They thought it was a promise that would not be fulfilled. So they complained against Moses and Aaron. They wanted to choose their own leader and return to Egypt.

With much disappointment at the attitude of the people, Moses and Aaron fell on their knees before them. Joshua, who had torn his clothes in a moment of grief, encouraged the Israelites to trust the Lord without fear because the Lord would make good on his promise. But the crowd's anger grew so intense that they wanted to stone Moses, Aaron, and Joshua.

Even today, the anger of protesters can turn into violence. We have seen them destroy buildings and loot small businesses. We pray that violence will come to an end and peace will be restored. We pray that all marches and demonstrations will be for the common good and be pathways for justice and peace.

Merciful Father, you call us to do justice. Strengthen us to be good citizens in our land and work to resolve inequalities through peaceful actions.

Hymn: "God of Grace and God of Glory," ELW #705. As we face evil and injustice in the world today, we sing to God to grant us strength.

Art: *Jews in the Desert*, Jacopo Tintoretto, 1593. What were some of the daily activities of the Israelites in this painting? Did life seem harsh? Who is the man with a halo at the lower right of this work of art? Do harsh living conditions lead to protests? (I could not find a work of art by the masters of the Israelites complaining, but this painting by Tintoretto provides a scene of life in the desert for God's first chosen people.)

Shopping Cart

I was hungry and you gave me food, I was thirsty and you
gave me something to drink.
—Matthew 25:35a

A call came from a shelter for abused women and their children. Since our
congregation had supported this ministry in the past, I was quick to help
again. The shelter was out of food. It was an emergency. What could I do
to feed those women and children, who lived safely at a location known to
few? I never knew exactly where these abused women and children lived,
but I was told the home was located in my part of the county.

I telephoned a retired member of my congregation to assist me in providing
food for these women and children in need. This retired member had a heart
for helping others, especially those who were disabled and/or oppressed.

I drove to her modest home, which was just a couple of miles from the
church. When she got in my car, we were off to the local supermarket to buy
the food. She took a shopping cart and filled it with many items—bread,
peanut butter, milk, canned vegetables, meats, and so on. She took her time
selecting healthy food.

By the time we stood in line at the cash register, her shopping cart was filled
with food like a horn of plenty. We took the groceries to the church, where
a counselor from the shelter picked the food up and restocked the shelves
for hungry women and children. There would be food on the table for those
who had been abused and needed to start over again in a safe place.

My church member who had done the shopping was pleased to help. She remained humble through it all and wanted no one to know what she had done. She wanted no praise, only the satisfaction that, as she helped the least in society, she did it as unto the Lord.

Emmaus Road

Matthew 25 tells the parable of the nations. On the last day, the nations of the world stand before the Lord for judgment. The faithful who fed the hungry, gave drink to the thirsty, welcomed the stranger, and visited the sick and those in prison will inherit the kingdom of heaven; those who did not will depart from the presence of the Lord.

May we see Christ in those who are hungry and oppressed as we respond generously and graciously. May our giving be genuine and done with humility. We do not want glory for our deeds; we give as the Lord has blessed us so that we remain faithful servants of Christ on this earth.

Living God, you bless us with many good gifts. May our hearts be open to share with others, quickly and humbly, what you have first given to us.

Hymn: "Lord of Glory, You Have Bought Us," ELW #707. Since God has abundantly blessed us, we freely and generously give to others.

Art: *The Miracle of the Loaves and Fish*, Jacopo Tintoretto, 1579–1581. Who are the two figures in the upper left-hand corner of this painting? What do you think they are saying to the boy between them, who is holding a basket of food? What is the mood of the people who are waiting to be fed? Does this painting help us to reflect upon global hunger and what can be done to alleviate the pains of those who are starving?

Powwow

For the Lord loves justice; he will not forsake his faithful
ones.

—Psalm 37:28

The Mowa Band of Choctaw Indians were a very poor tribe living in the
southern part of Alabama near the Gulf Coast. They were fighting for
federal recognition so they could receive financial aid. Before I arrived at
my congregation along the Gulf Coast, my congregation had already raised
funds to help this tribe purchase a tractor to farm their fields. That helped,
but there was much more ministry to be done to assist this tribe to raise its
standard of living.

I did not know just how poor this tribe was until the evening I drove my wife
and son to their powwow, which was twenty or so miles north of Mobile,
Alabama. As I drove to the powwow, my wife and I were shocked. We drove
on unpaved roads. The roads near the powwow were red clay. No concrete.
No blacktop. No gravel. As I drove, the tires of my car kicked up red dust
that clung to the windshield and body of my vehicle. The houses of these
Native Americans were shacks with boards of worn wood nailed together
for shelter. Who knows if they had indoor plumbing or potable water for
drinking and cooking?

They lived in poverty. I had never seen anything like this. We did not know
the plight of these Native Americans until that night. We had seen slums
before, but the living conditions of these Native Americans were at the
bottom of the economic barrel. Lord, have mercy.

At the powwow, we saw members of this tribe dressed in traditional clothing, including headdresses with colorful feathers. They sold handmade jewelry and delicious steamed, fresh corn in the husks. These sales were all to raise funds to help their community live from day to day.

In the midst of this powwow, the drumming grew louder and louder, and our ears began to hurt. My son, who was about two at the time, became frightened. He ran to me and raised his arms. I picked him up to comfort him as Native American men and women danced to the beat of the drums.

This powwow was something to behold: sights and sounds that we had never experienced before. It was an expression of their culture as they danced and celebrated in hope for federal recognition.

Emmaus Road

The Egyptian soldiers drowned in the Red Sea as they gave chase to the fleeing Israelites. God's people were safe. Their long journey to the promised land began with Moses, Aaron, and Miriam leading the way. We can just imagine Israel standing on the banks of the Red Sea and celebrating freedom. In Exodus 15 they sang of the Lord's triumph for them. Miriam and the women of Israel played tambourines and danced. In Exodus 15:21, Miriam sang of the victory the Lord had won for them with the words, "Sing to the Lord, for he has triumphed gloriously; horse and rider he has thrown into the sea."

When the oppressed are set free, isn't it a time for dancing? Isn't it a time for celebration? I pray that this Mowa Band of Choctaw Native Americans will win in court, receive federal recognition, enjoy a new life with a much higher standard of living, and have their dignity restored.

Lord of all nations, may we never forget those who fight for justice but remember their cries for help and assist them to improve their living conditions.

Hymn: "Blest Are They," ELW #728. This hymn takes the words of Jesus from the Sermon on the Mount and sets them to music to help us remember Jesus's promise of blessings for all who find themselves in those difficult moments of life.

Art: "Indians Dancing," Cornelius Krieghoff, 1855. What do you think might be the mood of those who are dancing? Can dancing stir the emotions of those who work for peace and justice? Can you think of spiritual moments with dancing and joy?

SECTION

4

Sorrow

Now Samuel died; and all Israel assembled and mourned for him.

—1 Samuel 25:1a

Homeless

> I was a stranger and you welcomed me.
>
> —Matthew 25:35c

He was one of the regular homeless persons who walked by our church. His gait was slow, and he was hunched over. He seemed to wander while looking for a warm and safe place to sleep or for a daily handout to buy fast food or an intoxicating beverage.

One Wednesday evening during Lent, my congregation gathered for a spaghetti supper that would be followed by worship. As we sat down to eat in our fellowship hall, he appeared at the door. I greeted him. He asked me to put him up for the night in a nearby motel. I had done so in the past, but I refused him that night. Instead I invited him to supper and then to attend worship.

He agreed. He ate his fill of spaghetti and then sat in the very back pew of the nave during the service. I occasionally glanced at him in that last pew. The service moved right along with prayers, singing, and biblical readings. As the last hymn was sung, I looked for him again. He was gone. Like a bird let out of a cage to enjoy a new freedom, he must have fled quickly.

I became anxious about his sudden disappearance. I wondered why he skipped out of the service so quickly. Didn't he want to ask me once again to pay for a night's lodging at the cheaply priced motels near the church? Didn't he want shelter from the cold?

When the service concluded, I shook the hands of the worshippers as they exited and made their way to their cars. A couple of ushers remained to turn off the lights, take care of the offering, and lock the doors.

To my shock, the offering plate was empty. No envelopes, no loose checks, no green dollar bills, and no silver coins were in sight. Our well-fed, homeless stranger of the evening was the culprit. Unnoticed by everyone, he had sped out of the church during the last hymn with the offering.

I guess I was too trusting of this homeless man, who had lost his way in life and did what he could to exist on the streets. He was welcomed by a genuine Christian spirit, but he turned that welcome into a moment of petty thievery. Although we had compassion for him, we did not expect our charity and love to be turned into a slap on our Christian faces.

Emmaus Road

Jesus commands us to care for the lowliest of society. Living an exemplary Christian life, Mother Teresa cared for the poorest of the poor in Calcutta. Congregations regularly gather offerings to support local and global missions. Almsgiving has always been central to the Judeo-Christian tradition.

In sacrificial giving, no one wants to be cheated. No one wants social service organizations to have high overhead while few of the offerings actually serve those in need. Givers give cheerfully to make a difference for those who are suffering. They know that giving can be risky at times, but they still take the chance to open their wallets and checkbooks for the sake of obeying the Lord, who inspires them to share with those in need.

Loving Jesus, you welcome us into your arms where we find peace and joy. Help us to welcome all people you send our way so that the love of Christ may be shared.

Hymn: "All Are Welcome," ELW #641. We are encouraged to create a house of faith to reach beyond its walls and touch the lives of strangers with the love of Christ.

Art: *The Most Welcome Visitor,* Eugenio Zampighi (date unknown but prior to 1945). Who is the visitor being welcomed? What are the indications that the family is welcoming him? How well do we welcome the stranger into our communities of faith?

Walking Home

Death has been swallowed up in victory. 'Where, O death is your victory? Where, O death, is your sting?' The sting of death is sin and the power of sin is the law. But thanks be to God, who gives us the victory through our Lord Jesus Christ.

—1 Corinthians 15:54b–57

Two middle school students walked home by a busy road one sunny September afternoon. They had walked along this narrow road many times and were aware that there were cars speeding along. They had been safe while walking home along this same route every day from school until that tragic day.

I don't know what really happened, but one of the boys, a member of my congregation, was hit by a car that day. His beautiful, happy, and innocent life came to a sudden and tragic end. His family and all of us at the church who knew him were devastated. The emotional shock really hurt. The driver was a mother who had her little child in the car with her. Oh, how she must have replayed that tragic moment in her mind and wondered what she could have done to avoid that tragedy!

When this accident happened, I had only been ordained a few years. I had officiated at several funerals of older members. Their deaths were more or less expected, but the tragic death of a child was totally unexpected. It was senseless. Emotions ranged from denial to shock to anger to grief.

At the visitation at the funeral home, people were respectful as they visited this boy's family. People whispered condolences to the boy's parents. There was a hushed tone in the room. There would be no raised voices. Shock took its toll. Who really knew what to say to bring comfort to this family that had lost a beloved son? But gentle hugs and the shedding of tears were signs of sympathy. The sting of death was still in the air. The question of where God was when this boy lost his life hovered over the crowd like a dark cloud on a stormy night.

Emmaus Road

We know there is shock and denial when we lose a loved one. Mary and Martha were grieving sisters when their brother, Lazarus, died. Martha believed that if Jesus had come sooner, her brother would not have died. Jesus could heal. He could restore life. Even though Lazarus had already been dead for several days and had been laid in a tomb, Jesus still defeated that enemy and raised his friend, Lazarus, from the dead.

Death was defeated. Lazarus was no lurching Frankenstein monster to frighten villagers. He was really set free through Christ's words to live again, breathe again, and love again. We who believe in Christ's promise of eternal life can shout with Saint Paul, as it is written in 1 Corinthians 15:55, "Where, O death, is your victory? Where, O death, is your sting?"

Victorious Savior, all praise and glory to your holy name, for you have defeated sin, death, and evil for people of every time and every place.

Hymn: "Thine Is the Glory," ELW #376. Raise your voice in praise to the Son of God, who defeated sin and death and gives us the joy of eternal life. With his triumphant resurrection, Christ makes good on his promise to overcome the grave for us all.

Art: *Resurrection of Christ*, Tintoretto, 1565. Who is adoring the risen Christ? Do they seem humble or amazed? How does Tintoretto depict the glory of the risen Christ?

Church Camp

> Now Moses used to take the tent and pitch it outside the camp, far off from the camp; he called it the tent of meeting. And everyone who sought the Lord would go out to the tent of meeting, which was outside the camp.
>
> —Exodus 33:7

I met him on a hot day at the gas station across the street from the church I served. He was tall, thin, unshaven, and tan from the sun's rays as he walked in the neighborhood. He wore walking shorts and a T-shirt. As I filled up my car with gas, he approached me and said, "I've pitched a tent on your church property."

I guess he recognized me as the pastor of the church across the street by my clerical collar and had seen me drive my car from the church parking lot to the gas station.

Surprised by the comments of this homeless man now camping in the dense grove of trees on my church's property, I asked, "What do you mean? Where did you pitch your tent?"

He replied, "It's over there in the trees." I quickly turned around and peered at that grove of trees along the church's driveway. It was difficult to see, but his orange tent was there among the tall pine and hardwood trees.

He told me that he had been camping there for a few days and would eventually move on. He had worked out a deal with the owner of the gas station to clean the station's parking lot and restrooms in exchange for bathroom privileges. After another moment of conversation, I gave him a few dollars to buy his lunch. I did not order him to move off the church's property immediately but gave him some time to think through his next move before packing up and going elsewhere.

He was homeless. He was a camper. He was trying to make his way in the world. He wandered from place to place while doing odd jobs. I assumed he would often have to depend on the goodwill of others to survive from day to day. He pitched his tent on the church's holy ground, a place of sanctuary, and sought help. I wondered if he knew that, in Hebrew scripture, it was told that Moses pitched God's Tent of Meeting in the midst of his people to be a gracious presence in their lives.

Emmaus Road

When I think of church camping, I don't immediately think of a homeless man pitching his tent on church property but of the church camps where children and adults enjoy the beauty of God's creation, take a break from the routines of daily life, and sing, pray, study, worship, play, rest, and breathe in a new perspective on life. Church camps encourage communing with the Holy Spirit.

In the wilderness, Moses pitched the Tent of Meeting, where the Lord dwelled among his people. In the first chapter of the Gospel of Saint John, we read that God, the Word, dwelled among us in Jesus. Another way to understand the word *dwell* in this context is to say that God pitched his tent among his people. When God camps among us, he is here to stay. His presence is abiding. God draws close to us in the midst of our lives, and we are welcomed by him.

Jesus, you who are the Word made flesh, dwell in our hearts so that we taste an abundant life in you.

Hymn: "Love Divine, All Loves Excelling," ELW #631. Where does God dwell? Does God dwell in some distant galaxy among the newly discovered planets, absent from this earth? In this hymn we sing for God to dwell among us.

Art: *Abraham and the Angels*, Rembrandt, 1646. Not finding an appropriate work of art for an image of the Tent of Meeting, I suggest looking at this painting from Rembrandt. Some may interpret this painting as a visit of the Trinity to Abraham and Sarah. Does this painting encourage us to reflect upon the presence of the Lord dwelling with us? What is Abraham doing? Who is watching the scene from behind the door? How is the glory or presence of the Lord displayed in this painting?

SECTION

5

Hope

Now faith is the assurance of things hoped for, the conviction of things not seen.

—Hebrews 11:1

Hospice Graduate

Jesus said to her, "I am the resurrection and the life. Those who believe in me, even though they die, will live, and everyone who lives and believes in me will never die. Do you believe this?"

—John 11:25–26

She boasted that she was the only graduate of hospice care because she had miraculously beaten cancer. Tooting the horn attached to her walker, this elderly, frail woman with gray hair, bright eyes, and a powerful voice maneuvered through crowds. Each Sunday at worship, I heard that horn as she made her way to her pew. She squeaked her way to where she wanted to go.

But cancer reoccurred in her body and finally took her. Her valiant fight for life ended. She entered into a new life promised by Christ for all the faithful at rest.

On that day that she died, my wife and I were drinking coffee at the breakfast table early in the morning. An unexpected beep broke the morning silence as we sipped our hot drinks. We were gently startled and asked one another, "What was that?"

We checked the smoke alarm, the only device we could relate to this strange sound. But the smoke alarm's battery was still good; it had not begun its repeated beeps of warning. And no, that beeping sound did not come from a washing machine, dryer, dishwasher, or refrigerator. So we sat at the kitchen table, perplexed and yet willing to forget the sound that had momentarily interrupted our quiet breakfast time.

A moment later the phone rang. Now that sound was familiar, but we wondered who could be calling so early in the morning. I answered the phone. To my shock, it was the hospice graduate's daughter. She spoke the sad words of her mother's death moments ago.

My wife and I never heard that single toot of that horn again. When I told her friends about the sequence of events at the breakfast table, one friend replied, "That was Sue giving you a toot on her way to heaven."

Emmaus Road

Reality TV produces shows about ghost whisperers and contacting the dead. These shows claim to reveal muffled voices from the underworld or shadows of ghosts moving swiftly from room to room. Some call these voices and shadows paranormal activities from the next life. Who really knows?

But one thing I do believe is Christ's promise when he said, "*I am the resurrection and the life.*" With faith in Christ, we rest in him until the day of his return. There is no need for more speculation about shadowy figures of the underworld or muffled voices from another realm—Christ promises immortality, glorified bodies, peaceful souls, endless joy, and true community with saints of every time and place. In the resurrected life, that hospice graduate will no longer need to toot the horn on her walker to make her way through the crowds of the faithful. There will be trumpets sounding praises to Almighty God, Father, Son, and Holy Spirit.

Eternal God, Father, Son, and Holy Spirit, as you gave life to your friend Lazarus, so give us that living water of life.

Hymn: "For All the Saints," ELW #422. Saints witnessed to their faith in Christ. Saints now rest from their labors. Saints will sing alleluias. With lives of faith, they receive the victory Christ won for them over the power of sin and death. As we sing with all the faithful, our voices join the saints of every time and place in glorious praise to the gracious God who created us, sustains us, and promises us life eternal.

Art: *The Resurrection of Christ*, Rembrandt, 1635/39. Which figure in this painting draws the most attention? How is Christ depicted? What was happening to the guards at the tomb? How did Rembrandt use bright and dark colors to communicate the message of this painting?

Divine Sign

When the steward tasted the water that had become wine, and did not know where it came from (though the servants who had drawn the water knew) … Jesus did this the first of his signs, in Cana of Galilee, and revealed his glory; and his disciples believed in him.

—John 2:9,11

I drove my 1964 aqua Pontiac Star Chief from St. Louis to Nashville to begin my studies at Vanderbilt Divinity School in preparation for ordination. I arrived in this southern city in the midst of five o'clock rush hour traffic. It was an August day, hot, sunny, and humid, and I dared not roll down the windows of my air-conditioned car.

I stopped at the red traffic light in the downtown area of Music City. I was lost. I had taken a wrong turn somewhere along the way and was on the wrong road to my apartment, which I had rented a few months earlier. I felt like finding the nearest gas station to pull over and ask for directions. After all, I could use a break from the six-hour trip from the Gateway City to the West. In Nashville, people said, I would find a church on every corner and musicians hoping to make it big, and I would soon experience southern hospitality.

As I waited for the traffic light to turn green, I glanced to my left and saw a stately stone church building with striking red doors. My eyes then drifted to the marquee in front of the church building. As God would have it, I saw it was a Lutheran church of my denominational preference. Now that was something familiar. But then I noticed the name of the interim pastor, who was my academic advisor at the divinity school. Now that was even better news for a young man embarking on his theological journey in a new town.

That downtown Lutheran church and my advisor's name on the marquee were signs of God's guidance. They were divine signs, giving me hope just when I was momentarily lost in a new town on my journey of faith. I was glad my eyes of faith had opened in the midst of bumper-to-bumper traffic to see that God was at my side.

Emmaus Road

Saint John's Gospel is sometimes called *The Book of Signs*. For example, John 2:1–11, containing the story of the miracle at Cana, is the first of Jesus's signs. All the signs in the Gospel of Saint John point to Jesus, who is the incarnate Word, filled with grace and truth. Jesus is the Word made flesh and enlightens us in this world of darkness (John 1:1–17). Jesus offered new life, healing, peace, and a joyful life for believers as his signs were made known in their lives.

Have we opened our eyes of faith and discovered signs of God's healing presence in our lives? As we open our eyes, we let go of the cares of this world and place our trust in the one whose cross and empty tomb are signs of eternal life for the whole world. Even when we find ourselves in frustrating and hopeless circumstances as we travel in the dark places of life, we open our eyes of faith and trust God. In so doing, we see divine signs, signs of God's presence, and signs of hope assuring us that God is by our sides to bring us life and light once again.

Jesus, bread of life, open our eyes of faith to see your presence in the loving deeds of life.

Hymn: "Peace Came to Earth," ELW #285. As we sing this Christmas hymn, we recognize that God is with us in the birth of the Messiah. He is with us as the wounded, dying Jesus on the cross. He is with us as we partake of Holy Communion. In an infant, in an innocent Man on the cross, and in the bread and wine of a sacred meal, we behold signs of God's deep love for us.

Art: *Scenes from the Life of Christ: 8. Marriage at Cana,* Giotto di Bondone, 1304–1306. Who are the three figures with halos? What is the servant woman doing with the large pitcher? Who is the figure listening to the man seated with a brightly colored halo? What do you think is Giotto di Bondone's message in this painting?

Good Job

> His master said to him, 'Well done, good and trustworthy slave; you have been trust-worthy in a few things, I will put you in charge of many things; enter into the joy of your master."
>
> —Matthew 25:21

In ministry there always comes time for evaluation. A congregation can review its ministry with a paid consultant or use volunteers from its own membership to do so.

Sunday after worship was one of those moments for members to remain seated to complete a brief evaluation of the congregation's ministry. There was one question to complete: "What can we do to improve our ministry?"

I shuddered to think of all the responses that might follow such a wide-open question. Some might write, "We need more justice ministries; we want more fellowship opportunities; the nave could use a different paint color; the pastor needs to shorten his sermons." Such responses may be helpful, some not, and some may even bring division within the congregation.

On that Sunday when the evaluations were distributed and completed, one survey caught my eye in particular. It came from a precocious little boy. He wrote, "Pastor, you are doing a good job. Don't change a thing."

I should have framed that survey. It would have given me an emotional boost when times got tough in the congregations I served. Sometimes, out of the mouths of babes, come honest thoughts.

Emmaus Road

Sometimes jobs can be satisfying. We joyfully use our God-given talents to do the best work that we can. But aren't there other moments when we feel that we are not using those talents to the best of our ability? In those moments, we just want to quit and walk away from the nine-to-five routine.

In Jesus's parable of the talents, the rich owner of a business gave each of his servants large sums of money (talents) to keep while he went away on a long journey. Perhaps the owner left to enjoy a long-awaited vacation to the Mediterranean beach or a visit with family members in another country.

Back home after his trip, he had an accounting with his servants. The two servants who invested the money and doubled its value were praised. Where could we invest today and see such dividend growth? But the slave who merely buried the master's money and kept it hidden in the ground was condemned for his laziness and lack of good business sense.

Haven't we heard of people hiding money in their television sets or in freezers, safe deposit boxes, or other places? The money may be safe for the future, but no monetary gains can be made in that kind of safekeeping.

We believe that God is the Creator and owner of all things, and we are called to manage wisely what he has first given to us—time, treasure, and talent. When the Lord calls for an accounting from us, may we hear those joyful words, "Well done, good and faithful servant."

Loving Lord, may we use our talents and gifts in service and to honor your holy name.

Hymn: "Lord, Whose Love in Humble Service," ELW #712. Following the humble and loving example of our Lord, we freely use our gifts to help others, including the sick, the hungry, and the oppressed.

Art: *Christ Washing the Disciples' Feet*, Tintoretto, date unknown. Whose feet is Jesus washing? What is the nature of their conversation? What are the rest of the disciples doing? Notice the halos on the heads of the disciples. What does this indicate? Does this painting call us to humble service following the example of Christ?

Long Walk Home

Assuming that he was in the group of travelers, they went
a day's journey. Then they started to look for him among
their relatives and friends. When they did not find him,
they returned to Jerusalem to search for him ... When his
parents saw him they were astonished; and his mother said
to him, "Child, why have you treated us like this?" ... He
said to them, "Why were you searching for me? Do you
not know that I must be in my Father's house?" ... Then
he went down with them and came to Nazareth, and was
obedient to them.

—Luke 2:44–45,48–49,51

Heinz was a boy during World War II and lived in Cologne, Germany.
For protection, he and many other German children were sent to school in
Austria. He never told me much about his time at this school, but his one
story about his time there is unforgettable. It is a story of faith.

At the end of World War II, the American military freed the children in
that Austrian school where Heinz and his two friends from Cologne had
found safe harbor. One day he and his friends plotted to leave that school
early in the morning and walk the hundreds of miles to their homes. Along
the way they would depend upon the hospitality of strangers who had
survived the war. It was a risk, but it was something these three boys vowed
to do to start life over again.

The day to leave arrived. The three boys woke up very early and began to
start their long journey home. But just before Heinz took a single step on

that road, he paused and told his friends he could not go through with their plan. He said that something inside him told him not to leave.

With saddened hearts, the other two boys left Heinz behind at the school. Heinz must have wondered if he would ever see them again and if he would ever make it back home to his family. Imagine the sadness and loneliness he must have felt when he said good-bye to his friends.

But then, as God would have it, hope entered Heinz's life. Within an hour of his friends' departure, Heinz's mother appeared at the school. I can just imagine Heinz saying that she was a sight for sore eyes. More than that, she was just what Heinz needed to break his utter despair. As Heinz told me this story about his mother showing up at the school to take him home, he commented, with his fervent faith, "That's God." Yes, Heinz, God never left your side. Yes, Heinz, God was there to bring love and comfort through your mother.

Heinz never saw his two friends again. Who knows what happened to them as they tried to make their way back home? We pray they found new and good homes somewhere else within Germany's borders.

That something inside Heinz, telling him to stay and not leave with his friends, was God's gentle whisper. God told Heinz to wait, be strong, and have faith. Heinz did so, and he lived to share his story of faith with many others, including his pastor. As we drank tea and ate cookies with his wife in the living room of their home one afternoon, Heinz told me his story.

Emmaus Road

When I was a child, I once found myself lost in a department store. I wandered away from my mother, who was shopping for a new dress. When I could not find my mother, fear took hold of me as never before. I finally found her among the dresses and blouses in that department store. Peace was restored.

On the way back to Nazareth from a pilgrimage to Jerusalem, Mary and Joseph realized that Jesus, their son, was not in the caravan. Like any devoted parents, they worried. They turned around and hastily headed back to Jerusalem to find their lost son. As they traveled, perhaps horrible thoughts came to mind. Had Jesus been attacked on the way home, and was he lying injured and bruised on the side of the road? Had kidnappers captured him and taken him to another part of the country to make him a slave? Jesus's parents probably never thought that their son was sharing his faith among the Temple leaders.

As Jesus matured and began his earthly ministry as an adult, he taught with parables. We recall the parable of the two sons—the prodigal son left home with his inheritance and was lost in loose living. Coming to his senses, he returned home, and his father welcomed his return. His son, who had been lost, was found. So we, who were lost in the clutches of sin and death, have been found in Christ to receive mercy, forgiveness, and grace. Now despair has lost its power, and the joy of being found in Christ prevails.

Almighty God, we cannot hide from you, nor would we want to. Find us and grant to us the inspiration of the Holy Spirit.

Hymn: "Go, My Children, with My Blessing," ELW #543. Baptized into Christ Jesus, forgiven by God's grace, and filled with the inspiration of the Holy Spirit, we are set free to go into this world to love and serve our neighbors.

Art: *Christ Among the Doctors*, Albrecht Dürer, 1506. Notice the variety of faces and expressions among the doctors in this painting. What moods does Dürer convey through their expressions? What are some of the doctors holding in their hands? How is the boy Jesus portrayed? What is the purpose of the gruesome-looking figure with a white head covering?

At the Lord's Table

> While they were eating, Jesus took a loaf of bread, and after blessing it he broke it, gave it to his disciples, and said, "Take eat; this is my body." Then he took a cup, and after giving thanks he gave it to them, saying, "Drink from it, all of you; for this is my blood of the covenant, which is poured out for many for the forgiveness of sins."
>
> —Matthew 26:26–28

Linda attended worship on Sundays with the congregation I served. She was an adult assistant at a local home that provided care for mentally and physically challenged adults. She and other assistants lived in the same large house with those adults who needed special care.

On occasion Linda brought two developmentally and physically challenged adults to worship with her. She bought Ruth, an African-American woman in her twenties. Ruth had big, brown eyes and a delightful smile. She had the reasoning power of a five-year-old, and whenever she saw me, she gave me a big hug.

Linda also brought Willy, a white male who appeared to be in his forties and who also had the mind of a child. Willy was frail. He never spoke. He limped along the aisle to his seat. He wore a brown protective helmet that looked like the helmet of a hockey goalie but had no face guard.

When it came time to commune during the worship service, all three of them came forward to kneel at the chancel rail. Linda carefully watched as Ruth and Willy took their places at the rail to receive the elements of this sacrament.

When I came to Ruth to give her the wafer, she looked up at me and smiled. She took the wafer and ate it as I said to her, "The body of Christ, given for you." Then I shifted a step or two and came to Willy. He took the wafer in his hand, lowered his head, and ate as I repeated those words of promise, "The body of Christ, given for you."

Along with Linda, their assistant, they ate and drank at the Lord's table. In faith, they received the real presence of the Lord Jesus Christ. They received a foretaste of the feast to come. It did not matter where they lived. It did not matter how old they were. It did not matter what they could or could not understand about this sacrament. All that mattered was that they came in faith, with humble and grateful hearts, to receive something special and holy.

Emmaus Road

I will never forget communing with them because it enabled me to realize even more that receiving this sacrament was not dependent on one's intellectual ability or status in life. Holy Communion is grace. It is a gift from the Christ who lived, died, rose, and ascended to give life to this broken and troubled world. All are invited to share in this joyful feast. All who are weary, struggling, guilt-ridden, sinful, and grieving are invited to come and share in Christ's promise of forgiveness, life, and salvation.

If receiving Holy Communion was dependent on knowledge alone or on one's moral stature, no one would qualify. Who can really discern or fully understand the divine mystery of Holy Communion? Who can be good enough to earn this divine gift?

Christ bids us to come. Christ speaks first. Christ gives us faith through the promised Holy Spirit. Christ calls us to eat and drink with grateful and joyful hearts. Linda, Ruth, and Willy came. They ate and drank at the Lord's table. Thanks be to God!

O God, the giver of every perfect gift, reveal your divine presence in this sacrament and assure us of your promise of salvation through Jesus Christ, our Lord.

Hymn: "Now the Silence," ELW #460. Communing at the Lord's table is a spiritual happening and joyful celebration. As we eat and drink, believing in Christ's promise of forgiveness, the spiritual boost happens in the present. It happens now.

Art: *The Last Supper,* Leonardo da Vinci, 1495–1498. Does Jesus seem to be welcoming his disciples with the opening of his hand? The disciples are painted in groups of three. Can you possibly identify them from what we know about them in the gospels? Does this painting encourage us to ponder Christ's presence in the sacrament of Holy Communion?

Poolroom Grace

For by grace you have been saved through faith, and this
is not your own doing; it is the gift of God—not the result
of works, so that no one may boast.

—Ephesians 2:8–9

The sign on the pole by a downtown street read, "No Standing 4–6 p.m."
Being new in town, I was not certain what that sign meant. I naïvely assumed
it meant *no loitering*. So I parked my car right next to that sign and walked
half a block with my friend, who had accompanied me to a downtown
bookstore so we could purchase our books for our first semester at the
divinity school.

All went well in the bookstore. We purchased our books and walked back
to my parked car. But when we arrived at that parking space on that busy
street, my car was gone. Had it been stolen? Where was it? I looked up
the street and saw a police officer writing tickets for parked cars. I told the
officer that I had parked my car just down the block and that it was gone.
With a stern look on his face, he said to me, "Can't you read the sign? No
Standing 4–6 p.m."

I was simultaneously embarrassed and angry. Of course, *no standing* meant
no parking. So I asked the officer where my car was located. He said it was
at the police impounding station, which was about a mile down the street.

With books in hand, my friend and I trudged down the street to the
impounding station. Once there, I looked through a chain-link fence, which
was eight feet high, and saw my 1964 aqua Pontiac Star Chief safely parked

with other impounded cars. I asked the attendant at the guardhouse how much it would cost to get my car released.

He glibly answered, "Twenty dollars."

I told him that I had no cash since I had just bought books for the semester. "Would you take a check?" I asked. But as soon as he saw my check was from an out-of-town bank, he said that he could not accept it. My friend offered to write a check for me, but the attendant said that would not work either.

With no cash and no checks good enough for payment, what was I to do? I could call a friend from the divinity school and ask him to pick us up. I could then go a local bank and cash a check for enough money to have my car released. Since this incident took place in the mid-1970s, before cell phones, I sought the nearest pay phone to make the call while my friend stayed at the impounding station.

Just down the street was a downtown dive, a poolroom where locals hung out for recreation. As I entered, it smelled of cigarette smoke and stale beer. Some locals sat at the bar, drinking their favorite brews, while others played pool. Growing up in a beer town and a neighborhood with a tavern on every corner, I had frequented those establishments with friends and family. Cigarette smoke, the smell of spilled beer on hardwood floors, and guys and gals gathering for conversation, pool, and card games were commonplace for me. So I felt comfortable as I walked over to the pay phone on the wall to make my telephone call. I had to pass the pool players.

"Hmm," I thought, "I played a lot of pool growing up. I just wonder if I could do some betting and hustle these guys." But I dropped that notion because I did not know the skill of my competitors; it would be foolish to challenge strangers. I would get no mercy if I lost and could not pay up.

So I did the next best thing. I told the truth.

"Excuse me, sir," I said to one of the pool sharks. "I'm new in town. I'm studying at the divinity school. My car was just impounded, and it will cost me twenty dollars to get it out. I need to get to the pay phone to make a call."

That pool shark, dressed in blue jeans and a plaid shirt, stared at me for a moment. He did not say a word. I guess he was deciding if my hard-luck story was true. Suddenly he reached into his back pocket, pulled out his wallet, and gave me a twenty-dollar bill. "It's for you," he said.

I was amazed. I was a stranger to him. I was a nobody. Yet he believed my story, and he was generous. He came to my aid. He gave me what I needed to release my car from impoundment. Now that was a gift. That was poolroom grace.

Emmaus Road

Grace is a gift and not a task. It comes as a surprise. It comes when you least expect it and from places unexpected. Divine grace saves us from the sinful condition of always being turned in upon ourselves. It saves us from greedy thoughts, hurtful words, and harmful deeds. Grace turns our lives around so that we can live for God and our neighbors. Grace shouts that we are loved even when we are unlovable.

In holy baptism, God's grace covers us from head to toe, washes away sin, incorporates us into the body of Christ, and sends us forth as missionaries empowered by the Holy Spirit. As one colleague told me long ago, "We don't have to do things because of God's grace; we get to do things." Yes, the things we get to do are works of love accomplished with joy and thanksgiving.

Eternal God, your grace is everlasting and abundant. We give you praise and thanks for this gift that we do not deserve and cannot earn.

Hymn: "In Thee Is Gladness," ELW #867. We sing alleluias to the victorious Lord, for he gives us joy and gladness. His grace opens our lives to praise him forevermore.

Art: *Carrying the Cross*, Peter Paul Rubens, date unknown. Who do you think may be wiping the brow of Christ on his way to the cross? Who is the person carrying the cross for Christ? Is there any significance to Jesus and the woman who wiped his brow both being dressed in black? Notice the two men being guarded by the soldiers at the bottom of the painting. Who are they? Does Rubens capture the chaos and agony on the way to the cross? Does the crowd seem sorrowful and sympathetic as they see Jesus on the way to his death? In his suffering and death, Christ offers us enduring and abundant grace.

A Church Builds

And I tell you, you are Peter, and on this rock I will build my church, and the gates of Hades will not prevail against it. I will give you the keys of the kingdom of heaven, and whatever you bind on earth will be bound in heaven, and whatever you loose on earth will be loosed in heaven.

—Matthew 16:18–19

To relocate a church is no small task. The congregation I served had contemplated a move to a different part of the metro area for a good ten years. Finally, when I arrived as the new pastor, it was time to put that plan into action. So the congregation embarked on a new spiritual journey that would take lots of faith and energy to relocate its ministry and to build some ten miles north of its present location on a major parkway across from a thriving high school.

While the new church building was under construction, the congregation rented space from a nearby middle school for Wednesday night activities and Sunday worship. Each Saturday, a crew of church members set up chairs and an altar in that middle-school cafeteria in preparation for Sunday worship. It was a long process, a long wait that tried our patience. But selling church property, buying new property, doing due diligence work, hiring the architect and contractor, attending zoning meetings, and constructing the new building took us about three years.

Those three years were a blessing to us from God. We arranged with the construction company to do some of the building ourselves to save money. Moreover, with the help of two local Baptist work crews, we framed our new church building and set up the trusses. One local painting company brought in their bucket truck to help us paint the highest parts of the interior of the building. Another local roofing company installed the shingles on the church roof without charge, and one more Baptist group helped us install drywall. Even our youth group got into the act as they learned how to frame the building with the help of talented carpenters. We even set up a large tent on our new property and ate breakfast and shared devotions together for two weeks with our Baptist brothers and sisters who helped us in the building process. It was ecumenism in action.

Just before the drywall was nailed into place, the congregation gathered one evening for prayer and reading of scripture. Then each member wrote his or her favorite Bible verse on the inner walls of the church building. If these church walls could talk, we would hear a variety of biblical promises shouting God's eternal love.

As members talked about the building process, it became apparent that God had provided miracle after miracle. Brothers and sisters in the faith worked long and hard to make ministry dreams a reality. Even some motorists who saw us constructing a new church stopped and gave us monetary donations. Truly God was in this place.

Emmaus Road

To build a church takes much energy, prayer, planning, and work. It takes time and patience. But building the church not only takes bricks, mortar, and hard hats, it also takes faith. It means being devoted to Christ and welcoming the Holy Spirit to lead the way to shape a new ministry in a new location.

For years I studied the literature of the church growth movement. So I helped committees publicize our church's ministry through various media outlets. Wearing out several pairs of shoes, I knocked on hundreds of doors in new neighborhoods. Congregational members helped me invite new residents to worship. I created brochures that highlighted our congregation's ministry to distribute to the church homeless. Mass mailings were also part of the publicity plan.

Guess what? Despite all that work, not many families joined the congregation I sought to build by knocking on doors and doing mass mailings. Certainly I visited new folks in their homes when they showed up for Sunday worship. But other new people came because members of the congregation invited them. It took friends inviting friends. It took relationship building to grow the church numerically.

Growing the church was not up to me and my efforts at evangelism alone. My call as the pastor was to share the gospel of Jesus Christ through the Word and sacraments, through teaching and counseling, and through prayer and holy conversations. Yes, I did my part with evangelism, but the growth of ministry was much more than what I did to reach out. The Holy Spirit empowered the members of the congregation to reach out to friends and neighbors, the church homeless, and strangers to share the love of Christ.

Through it all, I learned that God called me and others to plants seeds for ministry. It is God, through the Holy Spirit, who makes the church grow numerically and spiritually. It is God who builds his church, and I am only one of his servants.

In Genesis 6 we read that God called Noah to build the ark to save animals and humanity. Solomon was chosen by God to build the Temple where God dwelled because King David had to face much warfare, as it is written in 1 Kings 5. In Ephesians 2:20, Saint Paul reminds us the church is "built upon the foundation of the apostles and prophets, with Christ Jesus himself as the cornerstone."

A church builds through bricks and mortar. A church builds through the expansion of its ministry. A church builds through its leaders and laity. A church is built on faith in Jesus Christ. A church is built as we plant the seeds of ministry through the inspiration of the Holy Spirit. In the end, the church on earth prevails against the powers of evil as God has promised. It is God who builds his church through us.

Holy Lord, you promise that your kingdom will come and your church will stand against all powers of evil. Keep us holy and keep us faithful in the body of your Son, Jesus Christ, our Lord.

Hymn: "God Who Built This Wondrous Planet," Concordia Publishing House (text by Jaroslav J. Vajda and melody by Tom Leeseberg-Lange, 1986; setting, Bret Heim, 1996.) This strong hymn praises God, who built this earth and all things in the heavens. It also praises Christ, who builds his church on earth, and nothing will prevail against it.

Art: *Christ's Charge to Peter*, Peter Paul Rubens, 1614. What is Christ giving to Peter? What is Peter's posture as he receives this gift? Notice the bright colors in this painting. What moods do they express? What is the significance of Jesus being robed in white? What do the lambs in the lower right-hand corner of the painting symbolize?

Christmas with Katrina

Now in Joppa there was a disciple whose name was Tabitha, which in Greek is Dorcas. She was devoted to good works and acts of charity.

—Acts 9:36

A pastor in our mission trip group called it *Christmas with Katrina*. Lutheran pastors in St. Louis, adult leaders, and students from the middle school and high school spent the week after Christmas repairing homes and cleaning yards after the destruction left by Hurricane Katrina along the Gulf Coast in 2005. With the support of a Lutheran disaster relief agency and a nondenominational one, about twenty youths, several pastors, and a handful of adult leaders drove several hundred miles to Mobile, Alabama, for a week of ministry, fellowship, and worship.

When we arrived in this port city, we stayed at a church I happened to have served in the 1990s. Women and girls spent the night in classrooms while men and boys spread out their sleeping bags in the church's fellowship hall. We purchased groceries at a local grocery story, cooked at the church, and even shared a delicious seafood meal together at a restaurant near the bay.

But Mobile would not be the place where we plunged into ministry. We drove to a little fishing village outside of Mobile that *Forrest Gump* had made famous. Bayou La Batre, known for its fishing and shrimping industry, was devastated by the storm surge. Buildings were torn apart. With help from churches, good neighbors, volunteers, and the government, the community had to clean up and restore order.

In Bayou La Batre, we were divided into two groups with the assistance of a church disaster-relief agency. One group worked to repair a house that needed a set of outside stairs. A couple of youths remained on the ground for that job; other youths had to climb a ladder and squeeze through a window on the second floor of that house in order to paint its interior. I am sure that was an adventure for them.

The other group had to clean debris from the yard of another house and build a long privacy fence there. The work on the yard went well. However, when it came time to build the long fence, we needed the help of a carpenter to make sure the fence was straight and sturdy.

We worked for several days. No one got hurt except for one adult advisor, who stepped on a rusty nail that went right through her tennis shoe. After a tetanus shot and other medical care, she was fine and rested through the remainder of the trip. As our group worshipped together in the nave of the church where we stayed, we sensed a oneness in Christ and unity as a church in mission. God called us to be in mission to share his love with those who lost so much from the winds of destruction.

Emmaus Road

While in Joppa, as it is written in Acts 9:36, Saint Peter met a woman who was "devoted to good works and acts of charity." Tabitha, also called Dorcas, was a seamstress with a good heart. She made tunics and other clothing and shared them with poor widows who had little, if any, means of support. Since Saint Luke called her a disciple in Acts, she must have heard of Jesus and chosen to follow in his way. A result of her faith, she used her Spirit-given gifts to sew and make clothing to support herself and to share with those who had nothing. She was a self-made entrepreneur, charitable and faithful, and apparently made quite an impact in her community.

When Saint Peter heard of her death, he traveled from Lydda to Joppa. We can just imagine the scene when he encountered the deceased disciple. Widows were wailing and mourning. They told Peter about the clothing Dorcas had made for them. Moved by their grief, as we read in Acts 9:40, Peter knelt down, prayed, and then said to her, "Tabitha, get up." Miraculously, as when Jesus raised Lazarus from the dead, Tabitha rose. She stood up. She was alive again, could breathe again, could love again, and could once again be devoted to good works and acts of charity. The mission could continue for this beloved woman, who shared so much love with others.

The youths and adults who committed themselves to follow in the way of Christ and share his love received new life during our mission in Bayou La Batre. With sweat on their brows, with paint on their clothes, and with calluses on their hands, they felt the joy of being in mission for their Lord. Would they go again if they had the chance? You bet. As one adult advisor on the trip told me, "Pastor, if you decide to go again, let me know."

Almighty Father, Son, and Holy Spirit, keep us in mission so that the good news of Jesus's love may be spread to the ends of the earth.

Hymn: "We All Are One in Mission," ELW #576. We sing of the church's mission to spread the love of Christ as we share the various gifts from the Spirit.

Art: *Healing of the Cripple and Raising of Tabitha*, Masolino da Panicale, 1424. Does Saint Peter appear to be a Christ figure in this painting? Who is surrounding Tabitha? Does the color of the women's clothing symbolize grief and mourning? Does this painting give us hope that followers of Christ can be in mission and bring healing and good news to a weary world?

Acknowledgments and Copyrights

Scripture

Scripture verses quoted in each section follow.

Humor

Matthew 19:24
Psalm 33:3
John 12:21
Exodus 20:1–3
John 13:5a
Ephesians 5:8b
Matthew 19:14

Surprise

Luke 24:31a
1 Corinthians 9:16
Luke 2:8

Genesis 2:19a
Luke 10:19
2 Corinthians 9:7
1 Timothy 5:17
Romans 13:1
2 Corinthians 9:8
Luke 8:44

Justice

Isaiah 1:16–17
Hosea 12:6
Matthew 25:35a
Psalm 37:28

Sorrow

1 Samuel 25:1a
Matthew 25:35c
1 Corinthians 15:54b–57
Exodus 33:7

Hope

Hebrews 11:1
John 11:25–26
John 2:9, 2:11
Matthew 25:21
Luke 2:44–45, 2:48–49, 2:51
Matthew 26:26–28
Ephesians 2:8–9
Matthew 16:18–19
Acts 9:36

Stories

A member of the Heinz Schiefer family granted permission for me to use Heinz's name in "Long Walk Home." I appreciate the cooperation of this family. Heinz's story of faith and walking home with his mother at the end of World War II needs to be shared. I have had other members of my congregations who survived World War II as children and later shared their stories of faith with me. I wish I could tell them all, but many are too painful to tell. I appreciate these members and their witness of faith in Christ during very difficult times.

All names used in the stories are not real names except in the case of Heinz Schiefer.

There are no copyrights to list here. The stories I told are true, public, or known only to me in a personal way that I can freely share. I do not betray confidences from counseling sessions, and I do not share stories which may denigrate congregational members. I simply recall many memories of my parish ministry about God's people. I thank God for them all.

Emmaus Road Theological Reflections

I reflect theologically upon the theme of the scripture verses for each section to deepen knowledge and understanding of the Christian faith.

Hymns

Unless otherwise noted, all hymn suggestions in this book are found in *Evangelical Lutheran Worship*, Pew Edition, Copyright @ 2006, Evangelical Lutheran Church in America, Augsburg Fortress, Publishers. I have not copied any music or lyrics of the hymns but only referred to the page numbers of the hymns and their respective titles in *Evangelical Lutheran Worship*. Thus I did not need to secure any copyrights. I also included a brief comment for each hymn. I also suggested two hymns from Concordia Publishing House and did not copy any words or music.

The hymn suggestions in this book follow.

Humor

"Thine the Amen"
"Jesus, Come! For We Invite You"
"Let Us Ever Walk with Jesus"
"Christ Be Our Light"
"I Want to Walk as a Child of the Light"
"Draw Us in the Spirit's Tether"

Surprise

"Alleluia! Sing to Jesus"
"Where Shepherds Lately Knelt" (Concordia Publishing House, St. Louis, Missouri)
"God of the Sparrow"
"Healer of Our Every Ill"
"God, Whose Giving Knows No Ending"
"We Give Thee but Thine Own"
"This Is My Song"
"Praise and Thanksgiving"
"Thy Holy Wings"

Justice

"God of Grace and God of Glory"
"Lord of Glory, You Have Bought Us"
"Blest Are They"

Sorrow

"All Are Welcome"
"Thine Is the Glory"
"Love Divine, All Loves Excelling"

Hope

"For All the Saints"
"Peace Comes to Earth"
"Lord, Whose Love in Humble Service"
"Go, My Children, with My Blessing"
"Now the Silence"
"In Thee Is Gladness"
"God Who Built This Wondrous Planet," Concordia Publishing House. This hymn is one of my favorites. The text was written by Rev. Jaroslav Vajda, who was one of my pastors during my childhood; the tune was composed by Tom Leeseberg-Lange, who was a classmate in high school and college; and the setting was composed by Bret Heim, who was a choirmaster at a parish I served.
"We All Are One in Mission"

Art

In the early 1990s, when I served a congregation in Hoover (Birmingham), Alabama, I invited a fellow Lutheran, Dr. Frank McCoy, to lead a Wednesday evening program for Lent. Since Dr. McCoy was Chairman of the Fine Arts Department of the University of Montevallo in Montevallo, Alabama, his program during Lent focused on paintings of the masters that depicted Christ's passion through artistic skills. It was during that Wednesday evening program that I heard Dr. McCoy explain the idea that the masters who painted the scenes of Christ's passion story were not only artists but also theologians. They captured theological themes of the biblical story through light, darkness, colors, gestures, facial expressions, settings, and so forth.

For example, Rembrandt's painting *Supper at Emmaus* (1648), based on Luke 24, depicts the risen Christ with a halo. He is seated at table with two disciples. The halo emphasizes a holy and risen Savior, and the dark background provides a sense that he has risen from a tomb. His hands are breaking the bread, which symbolizes his presence in Holy Communion. These and other nuances point to theological themes that the masters provide in their works of art. I thank Dr. McCoy for sharing his insights and helping me to appreciate the biblical narrative through art.

Below are the artists with their respective art movements and the names of their paintings used in this book. All these works are in the public domain and can be found at www.the-athenaeum.org. Works of art are considered to be in the public domain seventy years after the artist's death.

On the Cover: Rembrandt van Rijn, *Supper at Emmaus*, 1648.

Section 1–Humor

Rembrandt van Rijn, *Musical Allegory*, 1626, Dutch Golden Age
Rembrandt, *Christ and the Woman at Samaria*, 1655.
Rembrandt, *Moses Destroying the Tablets*, 1659.
Tintoretto, *Christ Washing the Disciples' Feet*, 1548–1549, Italian Renaissance.
John Richmond, *Creation of Light*, 1826.
Lucas Cranach the Younger, *Christ Blessing the Children*, date unknown, German Northern Renaissance.

Surprise

Raffaello Sanzio da Urbino, Raphael, *Saint Paul Preaching in Athens*, 1515, Italian Renaissance.
El Greco, *The Adoration of the Shepherds*, 1610, Greek Mannerism.
Jan Brueghel the Younger, *Paradise*, circa 1620, Belgian Baroque.
Peter Paul Rubens, *Moses and the Brazen Serpent*, 1609–1610, Belgian Baroque.
Gabriel Metzu, *The Widow's Mite*, 1650–1652, Dutch Golden Age.
Rembrandt, *The Tribute Money*, 1635.

Rembrandt, *Saint Paul in Prison*, 1627.
Carl van Loo, *The Feeding of the Five Thousand*, 1733, Northern Renaissance.
Raphael, *Healing of the Lame Man*, 1515.

Justice

Tintoretto, *Jews in the Desert*, 1593, Italian Renaissance.
Tintoretto, *The Miracle of the Loaves and Fishes*, 1579–1581.
Cornelius Krieghoff, *Indians Dancing*, 1855, Dutch.

Sorrow

Eugenio Zampighi, *The Most Welcome Visitor*, date unknown, Italian.
Tintoretto, *Resurrection of Christ*, 1565.
Rembrandt, *Abraham and the Angels*, 1646.

Hope

Rembrandt, *The Resurrection of Christ*, 1635–1639.
Giotto di Bondone, *Scenes from the Life of Christ: 8. Marriage at Cana*, 1304–1306, Italian medieval.
Dirck van Baburen, *Christ Washing the Disciples' Feet*,
Albrecht Dürer, *Christ Among the Doctors*, 1506, German Northern Renaissance.
Leonardo da Vinci, *The Last Supper*, 1494–1498, Italian Renaissance.
Peter Paul Rubens, *Carrying the Cross*, date unknown.
Peter Paul Rubens, *Christ's Charge to Peter*, 1614.
Masolino da Panicale, *Healing of the Cripple and Raising of Tabitha*, 1424, Italian Early Renaissance.

I thank Monsignor Al Humbrecht for loaning me the following books to enable me to better understand the art of Rembrandt.

The Life, Times and Art of Rembrandt, Dr. Enzo Orlandi, General Editor, Copyright MCMLXVII, Crescent Books, a Division of Crown Publishing, Inc.

Rembrandt Paintings, Horst Gerson, Copyright 1968, Meulenhoff International, Amsterdam.

Rembrandt, Trewin Copplestone, Copyright 1964, the Hamlyn Publishing Group Limited, London, New York, Sydney, Toronto, Astronaut House, Feltham, Middlesex, England.

I also thank my longtime friend and colleague, the Rev. Barry Culbertson, for initially proofreading my work and providing editorial comments, and Deacon Michael Kucharzak for support through the publishing process.

Epilogue

In 2017 Catholics and Lutherans commemorate the five hundredth anniversary of the Reformation. This commemoration is the result of fifty years of ecumenical dialogue, which has produced theological papers such as the Joint Declaration of the Doctrine of Justification (1999).

Catholics and Lutherans are no longer condemning each other but are drawing closer in a common witness to Jesus Christ and demonstrating more unity in the one, holy, catholic, and apostolic church.

In my study of the documents from these ecumenical dialogues with Dr. Herbert Burhenn and from reading *The Annotated Luther, The Roots of Reform*, Volume 1 (Fortress Press, Minneapolis, 2015, Timothy J. Wengert, Volume Editor) and *Together by Grace: Introducing the Lutherans* (Augsburg Fortress, 2016, Kathryn A. Kleinhans, Editor), I have come to a deeper understanding of the traditions and doctrines of both Catholicism and Lutheranism.

I have learned that both of these branches of Christianity see scripture as holy, tradition as important, music and worship as essential for worship, and art as a way of deepening faith. Although some followers of Luther in the sixteenth century destroyed church art as a reaction against Catholicism, Martin Luther emphasized art as useful for teaching about the Christian faith. For Luther, scripture, hymns, and art were important features of enriching one's faith in Christ.

I hope that my work will be one small step in this ecumenical dialogue as I bring together scripture, stories of faith, theological reflections, hymns, and art that have historically served these Christian branches well in Christ's holy church.

In the Gospel of Saint Luke, chapter 24, the disciples on the road to Emmaus had their hearts spiritually burning and their minds spiritually enlightened as the risen Christ explained to them scripture about a dying and rising Messiah. In the breaking of the bread, those disciples recognized the presence of the victorious Lord.

As you read this book, may the Holy Spirit stir up your faith, inspire you to see a risen Lord working in your life, and encourage you to share your own story of faith with those God sends your way, as we are instructed in Luke 24:35: "Then they told what had happened on the road, and how he had been made known to them in the breaking of the bread."

In the name of God the Father, Son, and Holy Spirit.

Easter 2017

Printed in the United States
By Bookmasters